Big Book of
Juices and Smoothies

First published in 2009 by
New Holland Publishers (UK) Ltd
London • Cape Town • Sydney • Auckland

Garfield House
86–88 Edgware Road
London W2 2EA
www.newhollandpublishers.com

80 McKenzie Street
Cape Town 8001
South Africa

Unit 1, 66 Gibbes Street
Chatswood NSW 2067
Australia

218 Lake Road
Northcote
Auckland
New Zealand

10 9 8 7 6 5 4 3 2 1

ISBN 978 1 84773 548 5

Editor: Amy Corstorphine
Design: NHA and Vanessa Green
Production: Laurence Poos
Editorial Direction: Rosemary Wilkinson

Reproduction by Pica Digital Pte Ltd, Singapore
Printed and bound in Malaysia by Times Offset (M) Sdn Bhd

Publisher's note
The information given in this book is not intended as a
substitute for professional medical care. The publisher
and authors do not represent or warrant that the use of
recipes or other information contained in this book will
necessarily aid in the prevention or treatment of any
disease, and specifically disclaim any liability, loss or
risk, personal or otherwise, incurred as a consequence,
directly or indirectly, of the use and application of any
of the contents of this book. Readers must assume sole
responsibility for any diet, lifestyle and/or treatment
programme that they choose to follow. If you have
questions regarding the impact of diet and health, you
should speak to a healthcare professional.

   The publishers have made every effort to ensure
that the information contained in this book was
correct at the time of going to press, but medical
and nutritional knowledge are constantly evolving.
The authors and publisher cannot be held liable or
responsible for any form of misuse of any herb, herbal
preparation or so-called herbal remedy. You should
check with a qualified medical practitioner that the
product is suitable for you.

Big Book of
Juices and
Smoothies

130 delicious juices and smoothies to
enjoy throughout the day

Contents

Introduction

The *Big Book of Juices and Smoothies* is the book for you if you lead, or want to lead, a healthy lifestyle. There are 130 recipes devised to cater for your juicing needs from morning until night. But, most of all, *Big Book of Juices and Smoothies* is about taste. Each recipe is a celebration of global flavours which, thanks to the abundance of wonderful ingredients now available, are accessible to us all.

We weren't always juice and smoothie fanatics. Yes, there was a time when we innocently went about our lives thinking that a swig of juice from a carton was all the vitamin C we needed. However, this was before we bought juicers and blenders. Before we tasted sweet pomegranate juice. Before our cheeks glowed in the dead of winter. Before we were addicted to the beauty of juice and its benefits.

Eating fruits and vegetables is a vital part of a healthy, balanced diet, with many health organisations and nutritionists recommending that you should eat at least five servings a day. Eating a banana in the morning is an easy task, but having another four servings is another thing altogether. Yet we discovered, as our love affair with juices developed, that our daily requirements were already

being fulfilled, simply by sipping on exquisite juice and smoothie concoctions. Although the insatiable desire to explore uncharted flavour combinations was the initial driving force of our passion, the gifts that we received in the process became increasingly impossible to ignore. Soon we had thicker hair, glowing skin, cleansed bodies and boundless energy. Call us vain, but it was the "Damn, you look good" comments from those around us, that also kept the juices flowing.

Drinking fresh juices and smoothies isn't a new idea. Doctors and

naturopaths have been using fresh juices to treat patients since the nineteenth century. 'Juicing for health' pioneers, who hailed from Germany and Switzerland in the late nineteenth and early twentieth centuries, devised the Röhsaft Kur (the fresh juice cure), which is still practised today all over the world.

Then, many decades later in the late 1980s, the juicing craze hit California. Everyone was either setting up a juice bar or patronizing one. The success of juices in California is attributed to the abundance of local, fresh fruits, the 'take-away' lifestyle and, most of all, the importance Californians place on health and their bodies. It wasn't long before this craze swept across the rest of the USA, through Canada, across Europe and down to Australia, New Zealand and South Africa. Today, juice and smoothie bars – from über-trendy to naturally holistic – are everywhere. Juicing and smoothie-making has become a way of life.

Taking a walk down the Edgware Road in London, home to countless Middle Eastern restaurants, makes you question the true origins of juicing. There, amidst the bubbling pipes, tabbouleh and lamb kofta on a skewer, are giant juicers filled with fruit. You wouldn't even think of sitting down to a plate of kibbee without a tall glass of cantaloupe juice at your side.

"Fruit and vegetable juices are an essential part of our drinking culture in the Middle East," says food writer Anissa Helou. Juices are served from vendors along the streets, in cafés and in homes. When Helou was young, her mother would take her to the same café in Beirut every Saturday at noon, where she would perch on a stool and sip fresh carrot juice with her meal. "It wasn't a luxury item, it wasn't unusual, it was a healthy, refreshing part of daily life in a hot country."

Many of the drinks in this book are inspired by the flavours of the Middle East and celebrate its juicing tradition. As Helou said, juicing is a familiar part of their daily life. Familiarity breeds habit, so why not place a juicer and

a blender permanently on your kitchen counter so making juices and smoothies can become a daily part of your life as well? You'll have the freedom to experiment with a wide variety of fruits and vegetables, and to see, first hand, how they affect your body. As making juices and smoothies becomes a regular part of your life, not only will your body become healthier, your senses will grow sharper. Every sip, depending on the fruit, the vegetable, the variety or the season, becomes an exciting taste sensation. Some flavours are explosive, others are mild. Some tingle, others glide. Textures can be frothy or so thin they dissipate across the tongue. These intriguing taste-tests, which we conducted, are the inspiration behind the descriptive word included with each recipe. Putting a single word to each flavour, however, wasn't always on the tip of the tongue. Flavours are often difficult to describe, says Mark Miller, an American food writer, restaurateur and chilli pepper expert. He says, "Taste is an existential, sensual experience. We really don't understand it. Language is what we use for taste, and yet the body goes through this temporal process; there are highs and lows, intensities and durations. Taste is a very, very complex thing in the body." Using language to describe taste, Miller explains, is analytical, and not always about the experience itself. Our descriptive words are therefore mere guidelines – we will leave you to come up with your own once you've sampled your juices and smoothies.

Let's get started!

Juicers and blenders

Juicers and blenders aren't simply for health junkies or kitchen gadget lovers. Juicing is a quick and healthy habit that can be worked into your daily routine, regardless of how busy you are. The first thing you need to do is invest in the right equipment. Whether it's citrus fruits, carrots, wheatgrass or a blend of all three that you're after, there's a juicer or blender out there that's perfect for you. Note that for many of the recipes, you will need a juicer and a blender, and for some, a cocktail shaker.

Quality costs

The higher the wattage of the juicer, the more efficient and expensive it will be. Wattage varies greatly from juicer to juicer. The first thing you need to do is decide what kind of juice you want. Do you want a pulpy, fast product or a crystal clear liquid? Do you want to juice dense, fibrous vegetables or soft, tender kiwis? The harder the grinding job, the more powerful and durable the juicer will need to be (think juicing a turnip versus a blackberry). Domestic juicers can have a wattage as low as 200, while industrial juicers can have well over 1000 watts. It is important to decide from the start

how serious you are about juicing, keeping in mind that most of us don't need an industrial juicer strong enough to juice a small tree. Juicing is an investment in your health, which, of course, is priceless.

As well as considering how much you want to spend, there are a few other things to take into consideration:

- Always look out for a juicer with a stainless steel blade, not aluminium, which rusts more easily and can taint your food.

- Look for a feed tube that is at least large enough to fit a whole, large carrot. It's no fun chopping your fruits and vegetables into matchsticks in order to get them into the juicer.

- Look for a juicer with a cup large enough to accommodate at least 500ml (18fl oz) of juice.

- Make sure there is a sufficiently sized compartment in the juicer to collect pulp as you juice. Some juicers have an external container to collect pulp, which means you can juice longer without having to stop and de-clog.

Juicing methods

There are three basic types of juicer: centrifugal, masticating and press. Whatever type of juicer you have, always remember to clean it and your workspace thoroughly after use. A tidy kitchen results in a tidy mind – you will function more efficiently in your day and also inhibit the growth of any germs or bacteria.

Centrifugal juicers

Most, if not all, of the cheaper domestic juicers fall into this category. Centrifugal juicers work by first

grinding the fruit and vegetables, then spinning them at very high revolutions per minute (RPM), somewhat like a washing machine. The juice runs out and the pulp is ejected into a separate container. Centrifugal juicers are not generally recommended if you want a high-quality juice on a daily basis. The end product is quite thick and cloudy, contains a lot of pulp, and enzymes can be destroyed in the juicing process. But, with the additional citrus and blender attachments often available with these juicers, they are an affordable way to start juicing.

Masticating juicers

The second most expensive type of juicer on the market. Masticating juicers operate at a slower speed than centrifugal juicers. They masticate by chewing up fruit and vegetable fibres and breaking down their cell structure. Masticating juicers perform better with fibrous fruit and vegetables than centrifugal juicers. The quality of the end product is high and more juice is removed from the pulp than from a centrifugal juicer. This produces a clearer, less cloudy juice, which is more nutritious as it retains more fibre, enzymes, vitamins and trace minerals in the finished product. More expensive masticating juicers often come with additional homogenizing units that make baby foods, sauces and fruit sorbets.

Press juicers

Press juicers are the most efficient and, consequently the most expensive, juicers you can buy. Press juicers work by first crushing the fruit and vegetables and then pressing them, much like the press used to make extra virgin olive oil. They are typically the slowest of the juicers (turning at a slower RPM) which creates little friction; therefore no heat is applied to the fruit. Press juicers produce by far the best quality juice. The process gives you more fibre, enzymes, vitamins and trace minerals than any other method. The nutritional value of pressed juice is so high that it is often used as a medicinal supplement for patients, especially those suffering from cancer. Some press juicers have the additional

function of magnetic and bioceramic technology. This is beneficial as it slows down the oxidation process, meaning juices can be stored for longer (three days maximum).

Blenders

A blender is what you will need to make smoothies. Yogurt, milk and ice, along with other ingredients, can be added to blenders and the result is a smoothie, shake or ice crush. Blenders are generally cheaper than juicers. Hand blenders are also readily available on the market and require less cleaning. Blenders, as their name suggests, blend fruits and vegetables together rather than extracting juice So if you prefer a thicker, pulpy, more textured fruit or creamy drink like a smoothie then a blender is all you

require. However, if pure juice is want you want, separated from pulp, a juicer is what you'll have to buy.

Other useful equipment

In order to make your juicing and smoothie-making experience as easy and as enjoyable as possible, we recommend investing in a few extra tools.

Apple corer – this little gadget makes coring apples and pears a much easier and quicker job than doing it with a knife.

Cannelle knife – this works in a similar way to a zester, but you get much longer ribbons of zest.

Cherry stoner – takes the hard work out of pitting cherries.

Chopping boards – useful when preparing fruit and vegetables.

Cocktail Shaker – useful for blending ingredients, particularly those of different consistencies, like cream and fruit juice. A few cubes of ice inside act as beaters and slightly dilute the ingredients. Cocktail shakers are usually fitted with strainers, so you can pour the drink while keeping the ice cubes behind.

Fine sieve or muslin – essential for straining unwanted pulp or ingredients.

Fine wire brush – for cleaning your juicer.

Glass jars with lids – these are great for storing and transporting your juices and smoothies. Don't forget to shake before drinking.

Ice cream scoops – these will help you scoop ice cream, frozen yogurts and sorbets easily. A tip: dip the ice cream scoop into hot water between each scoop as this will stop the ice cream from sticking.

Ice-crushing machine – this isn't an essential piece of equipment, since many blenders and smoothie makers will do the job. To crush ice by hand lay a clean cloth on a work surface. Spread ice cubes over one half of the cloth and fold the other half over to

Plastic spatula – ideal for scraping thick blends out of your blender.

Scales – if you want to make juicing a science then scales are essential. Don't forget you can and should be experimental while juicing – use what is in season or what you have in your fridge. Make substitutions and adjust the recipes to suit your own taste buds – the recipes are only a guide!

Scrubbing brush – make sure you remove all the dirt from your fruit and vegetables by washing or scrubbing.

Sharp knives – good, sharp knives are important in any kitchen and for any task. Make sure your knives are sharpened on a regular basis, preferably by the same person.

cover the ice. Use a heavy implement, such as a mallet, to crush the ice, striking firmly. Unfold the cloth and, with a spoon, scrape the crushed ice lightly away from the cloth. Transfer the crushed ice to a jug or glasses.

Lemon squeezer – keep one of these in the cupboard. They are invaluable for producing almost instant citrus juice to add to recipes.

Measuring jugs and spoons – it is useful to keep a selection of these handy.

Plastic milk/juice containers – recycle these for freezing 'pure' juices e.g. apple, pear, melon and tomato.

Small whisk – use to combine different juices.

Vacuum flask – this is the more expensive alternative to glass jars. .

Vegetable peeler – use only when necessary. Most of the nutrients in fruits and vegetables are in the skin.

Zesters – these are useful for grating the rinds of citrus fruits to add to recipes and also to create swirls of rind to use as garnishes.

Juicy Ingredients

The drink that comes out of your juicer or blender will only be as good as the ingredients that you put in. Try to shop with this in mind. If you're making a healthy juice it makes sense to avoid fresh produce that is likely to have been sprayed with pesticides. If you're making an indulgent smoothie don't use poor-quality yogurt or ice cream that's going to be lacking in that all-important creamy taste and texture. If you're going to take the time to make your own drinks, make them as good-quality as they possibly can be.

Fruit and vegetables

The fruit and vegetables you use in your juices and smoothies will have a massive impact on the flavour of your drink and its quality. Try to remember these few simple points when you are buying your ingredients:

- Buy seasonal fruit and vegetables whenever possible.

- The riper the fruit is, the sweeter the resulting flavour. It will also give a better yield.

- Ensure that the produce is unblemished.

- Buy organic produce where possible as it is pesticide-free, purer and better for you. If you are not using organic ingredients you can peel the fruits and vegetables prior to using them in a recipe if you prefer.

- For convenience (and if fresh produce is unavailable), dried, canned, frozen or bottled fruit and vegetables can be used. Opt for the best quality you can find.

- When soft fruit is in season, large quantities can be purchased and frozen for use later.

Preparation

There are a few simple things that you need to bear in mind before using the fruit and vegetables:

- All fruit, vegetables and herbs should be washed before use.

- The fruits and vegetables that you use should not only be as fresh as possible, but also visually perfect. This means they should be free from all blemishes and bruises and not over-ripe.

- Fruits with inedible skins, such as bananas and mangoes, should be peeled before use.

Hard fruits – you will need to use a juicer for hard fruits, such as apples and pears. Cut them into quarters and remove the stems.

Soft and stoned fruits – these can be juiced using a blender or food processor.

- Make sure you de-stalk berries where needed.

- Remove stones before using.

Dried fruits – these need to be soaked for a few hours in hot water to re-hydrate them prior to use.

Root and tuber vegetables – these must be juiced using a centrifugal or masticating juicer.

Dairy and non-dairy produce

The same rules apply – buy the best quality that you can, organic wherever possible.

Semi-skimmed/skimmed milk – opt for these if you want a healthier drink or are counting the calories. They are calcium-rich but lower in fat and calories than full-fat milk.

Full-fat milk – rich and creamy but high in saturated fat.

Cream – for indulgent recipes and treats, a variety of creams may be used e.g. single or double.

Creamy fat-free yogurt – fat-free and low in calories.

Live bio yogurt – this can help improve the digestive system as it contains healthy bacteria. It is rich in calcium and is often suitable for those who suffer from lactose intolerance.

Greek yogurt – this is much thicker than standard varieties of yogurt but it is extremely high in calories and should therefore only be used for the occasional treat. Lower-fat options are available.

Reduced-fat coconut milk – a good alternative to fuller-fat varieties.

Almond milk – a non-dairy alternative, low in cholesterol and with no added sugar. Suitable for vegetarians and rich in mono-unsaturated fats.

Rice milk – this has a thinner consistency to cow's milk and has a very sweet flavour. Rice milk also comes in a variety of flavours, such as chocolate and vanilla.

Soya milk – a non-dairy alternative to cow's milk and gluten-free.

Oat milk – an alternative to cow's milk, with a rich, creamy and smooth taste.

Buttermilk – high in calcium, low in fat and an aid to digestion.

Ice cream – virtually every flavour imaginable is now available. There are also many low-fat, low-sugar and similarly health-conscious varieties on the market too. Buy the best quality ice cream that you can afford.

Tofu – also known as soya bean curd. Tofu comes in three different textures – firm, medium-firm and silken. Because tofu is naturally bland, it will affect the texture, rather than the taste, of the drink. Silken tofu is the best variety to use when blending because of its creamy, thick texture.

19

Natural additions

I'm sure that you will be familiar with most of the ingredients used in this book, but there may be a few, such as some natural additions that may be new to you. **The important thing to note about these additions is that they must be used according to the manufacturers' instructions and you should check that the product is suitable for you.**

Bee pollen – considered to be one of nature's most complete foods, bee pollen contains all 22 amino acids, minerals, vitamins and enzymes. It's a great energy booster, a source of protein and can help reduce the effects of stress.

Echinacea – stimulates the immune system and the lymphatic system. Echinacea comes in capsule, extract and tea forms.

Flaxseed oil – useful for vegetarians and non-fish eaters. Rich in omega-3 essential fatty acid, alpha linolenic, and can be converted in the body to the fatty acids EPA and DHA, which are those present in fish. Said to reduce the risk of heart disease and other ailments. Flaxseeds are available in ground form and as oil.

Spirulina – a microscopic algae in the shape of a coil. Now being called a 'superfood'. Contains the highest concentration of nutrients known in any one food, plant, grain or herb. Available to buy in powder and capsule form.

Wheatgerm – an excellent source of B vitamins, vitamin E, folic acid, iron, magnesium and potassium. Available in flaked form or as an extracted oil.

Wheatgrass – the grains of wheat that have sprouted until they become young grass. It is said to be cleansing and boosting to the immune system – an all-round tonic.

Top Tips

- Make sure that your juices and smoothies are cold when served.

- Juices and smoothies are made for drinking immediately. Their nutritional value decreases the longer they are exposed to air and some fruit and vegetable juices tend to separate quickly. It is therefore not advisable to store them for more than 1 day.

- If your smoothie is too thick, water it down with still mineral water or another fruit juice (apple is a good mixer); if it is too thin add yogurt for extra body.

- Drinks that are too tart can be sweetened with a little clear honey.

- Experiment with different fruits and vegetables to make your own unique drinks. Make sure you don't use too many ingredients in any one recipe however, as this will overpower the drink and mask individual flavours.

- In general you need to take care when mixing fruit and vegetable juices – some can cause flatulence or bloating. The exceptions to this are carrot and apple, which are very good mixer juices in themselves.

- Freeze puréed fruit in ice cube trays and use the fruit ice cubes to add additional flavour to your drinks.

- Frozen fruits work extremely well in smoothies.

The Look

Presentation probably isn't going to be your top priority if you're drinking your juice or smoothie first thing in the morning before rushing off to work, but if you have friends staying for the weekend or are hosting a family brunch party, it's fun to serve up something that looks special.

Class in a glass

There is a huge array of glassware available, in every colour, size and shape imaginable. Plastic picnic glasses have also become very stylish – perfect if you're planning an al fresco dining experience. Even fun paper cups, with spotted and striped designs, can look great in the right context. Do think carefully about which glass your drink will look best in, and try to stick to clear glass wherever possible. Many of the drinks featured in this book won't look particularly great if poured into coloured glasses: the combination of the colour of the glass and the colour of the juice can sometimes produce a murky-looking result.

Stir it up

Cocktail swizzle sticks, straws, little umbrellas and long-handled spoons all make good accessories for your drinks. They are particularly fun additions if you're serving them at a party or picnic.

The finishing touch

The kind of garnish that you choose will obviously depend on what type of drink you're having and the ingredients it contains, and it will also to some extent be dictated by the context in which you are drinking or serving it. Obviously, it would not be sensible to top a healthy pure fruit juice with crushed chocolate cookies. Similarly, you wouldn't finish off a luxurious ice cream smoothie with a sprinkling of wheatgerm. Here are just a few ideas – slices of fruit, citrus curls, herb sprigs, nuts and berries for the healthy option and crushed cookies, grated chocolate, flavoured sauces or a scoop of ice cream for moments of indulgence.

Important Notes

- Each recipe makes one drink or serving.

- Those new to drinking pure fruit and vegetable juices and smoothies should drink no more than two servings a day.

- Four servings a day is the maximum for a more seasoned drinker. For maximum nutrient intake, vary the fruits and vegetables you use.

- You must always dilute 100-per cent pure fruit and vegetable juices and smoothies that are to be served to children. Still mineral water is best for this, but you could use lemonade, sparkling water, soda or milk, as appropriate.

- If using herbal remedies or supple- ments always read the information supplied by the manufacturer to check that the product is suitable for you. If in doubt, consult a medical practitioner. Omitting the herbal supplements will not affect the flavour or overall quality of the drink.

- Consult your doctor before taking any supplements at all if you are pregnant, breast-feeding, elderly or taking any prescribed medicines.

• Beetroot should only ever be used in small quantities and should never be drunk as a juice on its own as it can cause stomach upsets and nausea.

• You should always consult your doctor before drinking large quantities of grapefruit juice if you are taking prescribed medicine.

• Do not use the leaves of rhubarb as they are poisonous. You should always cook rhubarb before eating it or adding it to a recipe because of the high levels of oxalic acid it contains.

Standard weights

1 bunch ALFALFA SPROUTS
10g/½oz
1 APPLE cored and quartered
150g/5oz
1 APRICOT stoned   50g/2oz
1 AVOCADO peeled and stoned
125g/4oz
1 BANANA peeled   100g/3½oz
1 BEETROOT with leaves 100g/3½oz
1 handful BLACKBERRIES (fresh/frozen)
50g/2oz
1 handful BLACKCURRANTS stalks
removed (fresh/frozen)   50g/2oz
1 handful BLUEBERRIES (fresh/frozen)
50g/2oz
1 baby CABBAGE (red/white) outer
leaves removed   400g/14oz
1 CARROT top and bottom removed
100g/3½oz
1 stalk CELERY trimmed, with leaves
50g/2oz
1 CELERIAC peeled   300g/10½oz
1 handful CHERRIES stoned and stalks
removed   50g/2oz
1 head CHICORY   160g/5½oz
1 fresh CHILLI   5g/¼oz
1 bunch CORIANDER chopped
10g/½oz
1 handful CRANBERRIES (fresh/frozen)
50g/2oz
1 CUCUMBER   500g/1lb
1 FEIJOA flesh scooped out
75g/2½oz
1 FENNEL bulb outer part removed
225g/8oz
1 FIG   40g/½oz

1 clove GARLIC peeled   5g/¼oz
1cm (1/3in) piece fresh GINGER
peeled   5g/¼oz
1 handful GOOSEBERRIES
(fresh/frozen)   50g/2oz
1 bunch GRAPES (red/white) stalks
removed   200g/7oz
1 GRAPEFRUIT (ruby red/white) peeled
200g/7oz
1 ICEBERG LETTUCE outer leaves
removed   550g/1lb3oz
1 KIWI FRUIT   75g/2½oz
1 LEEK trimmed   100g/3½oz
1 LEMON peeled   75g/2½oz
1 stalk LEMONGRASS trimmed and
chopped   10g/½oz
1 LIME peeled   50g/2oz
1 LYCHEE   10g/½oz
1 MANGE TOUT (snow peas)   1 tsp
1 MANGO peeled and stoned
225g/8oz
1 MELON (green/cantaloupe) peeled
and deseeded   200g/7oz
1 NECTARINE stoned   75g/2½oz
1 ORANGE (blood orange) peeled
150g/5oz
1 PAPAYA peeled and deseeded
150g/5oz
1 bunch PARSLEY woody stalks
removed   10g/½oz
1 PASSION-FRUIT flesh scooped out
30g/1oz
1 PEACH stoned   150g/5oz
1 PEAR cored and quartered
150g/5oz
1 PEPPER (red/green) stalk removed,
deseeded   125g/4oz
1 PERSIMMON peeled   50g/2oz

1 PINEAPPLE peeled   900g/2lb
1 PLUM (including greengage) stoned
                      50g/2oz
1 POMEGRANATE seeds scooped out
                      100g/3½oz
1 QUINCE peeled and quartered
                      200g/7oz
1 head RADICCHIO outer leaves
removed   50g/2oz
1 RADISH with leaves   7.5g/½oz
1 handful RASPBERRIES (fresh/frozen)
                      50g/2oz
1 bunch ROCKET   25g/1oz
1 SAGE LEAF   1 tsp
1 bunch SPINACH tough stalks
removed, chopped   50g/2oz
1 SPRING ONION trimmed
                      10g/½oz
1 SQUASH peeled, deseeded
                      300g/10½oz
1 handful STRAWBERRIES hulled
                      100g/3½oz
1 SWEET POTATO peeled
                      200g/7oz
1 TAMARILLO flesh scooped out
                      50g/2oz
1 TOMATO stalks removed
                      75g/2½oz
1 handful WATERCRESS   50g/2oz
1 WATERMELON flesh and seeds
scooped out   2kg/4lb
1 handful WHEATGRASS rinsed and
chopped   10g/½oz

Just Fruit

Cherry Delight

1 apple, quartered and cored

1 pear, quartered and cored

50 g/2 oz cherries, stalks removed and stoned

Ice cubes to serve

Fresh mint sprig to garnish

1. Juice the apple, pear and cherries together.

2. Pour into a glass over ice. Garnish with a mint sprig.

Summer Breeze

1 orange, peel removed and quartered

200 g/7 oz black grapes, stalks removed

1 pear, quartered and cored

Ice cubes to serve

Twist of lime to garnish

1. Juice the orange, grapes and pear together.

2. Pour into a glass over ice.
Garnish with a twist of lime.

Red Velvet

1 pomegranate, cut in half and seeds

scooped out

175 g/6 oz raspberries

1 tsp rosewater

1. Juice the fruits and stir in the rosewater.

2. Serve in a shot glass.

Summer Sunset

1 pomegranate, cut in half and seeds
scooped out

1 orange, peeled and quartered

Crushed ice to serve

2 tsp orange flower water

1. Juice the fruits separately.

2. Pour the pomegranate juice into
the glass first over crushed ice.

3. Top with the orange juice and stir in
the orange flower water.

Mango Lassi

100 ml/3½ fl oz still mineral water, chilled

1 mango, halved either side of the stone, the flesh
scooped out and cut away from the stone

110 g/4 oz natural yogurt

Pinch of cinnamon

Sliced mango and cinnamon stick to garnish

1. Place all of the ingredients in the blender
    and blend until smooth.

2. Pour into a glass and garnish with sliced mango
    and a cinnamon stick.

Ruby Reviver

1 blood orange, peeled and quartered

1 lime, peeled and halved

**1 passion fruit, cut in half and the
pulp scooped out**

Ice cubes or crushed to serve

1. Juice the orange and lime together.

2. Stir the passion fruit pulp into the juice.

3. Pour into a glass over ice.

In the Pink

1 pink grapefruit, peeled and quartered

75 g/3 oz cranberries, fresh or frozen

1 apple, quartered and cored

Ice cubes or crushed ice to serve

1. Juice together the grapefruit and cranberries, then add the apple and blend together.

2. Pour into a glass over ice and serve chilled.

Grape Surprise

200 g/7 oz red grapes, stalks removed

200 g/7 oz white grapes, stalks removed

1 apple, quartered and cored

6 fresh mint leaves (apple mint is nice)

Ice cubes or crushed ice to serve

1. Juice together the grapes and apple.

2. Stir in the mint leaves. Pour into a glass over ice.

3. For a long, cool drink dilute
   with sparkling mineral water.

Caribbean Dream

2 bananas

1 medium mango

1 medium pineapple

200 ml/7 fl oz coconut milk

Pineapple wedges and lime, to garnish

1. Peel the bananas and cut into three or four pieces.

2. Cut the unpeeled mango flesh away from the stone. Peel the pineapple and cut into chunks.

3. Juice the mango and pineapple together, pour into a blender, add the banana and coconut milk and liquidise until smooth.

Guava Buzz

- -

6 guavas

10 apricots

2 pears

Crushed ice

1. Halve the guavas. Halve the apricots and remove the stones. Twist the stalks off the pears and cut into quarters.

2. Juice all the fruits together.

3. Serve poured into glasses over crushed ice.

Just Peachy

4 mandarins

2 yellow flesh peaches

Seeds of 1 pomegranate

**Borage flowers,
to garnish (optional)**

1. Peel the mandarins. Halve the peaches and remove the stones. Cut the pomegranate in half across the centre and pop out the seeds with a skewer or the point of a knife.

2. Juice the mandarins and peaches, pour into glasses and drop in the pomegranate seeds. Float a few borage flowers on top of each serving for a pretty final flourish.

Purple Haze

½ Ogen or Galia melon, about 400 g/14 oz,
plus extra to garnish

1 passion-fruit

115 g/4 oz blueberries

175 g/6 oz blackberries

1. If using Ogen melon, leave it unpeeled, if
using Galia, cut away the skin. Cut the melon into
chunks, setting aside a few extra slices for decoration.
Halve and scoop the pulp and seeds out
of the passion fruit.

2. Juice all the fruits together, including the
passion fruit seeds, pour into glasses and
serve with the melon slices to garnish.

Pink Lady

1 ruby red grapefruit, peeled

1 white grapefruit, peeled

1 handful cranberries

1. Juice the grapefruits and cranberries together.

Suspended Passion

2 oranges peeled and halved

1 banana, peeled

1 passion-fruit pulp, scooped out

1. Juice the oranges. Blend with the banana and stir in the passion-fruit pulp.

Sunny Morning

· ·

3 ice cubes

1 pear, peeled, halved, cored and chopped

3 apricots, halved, stoned and chopped

1 nectarine, halved, stoned and chopped

100 ml/3½ fl oz pear juice

Extra sliced apricot and nectarine to garnish

1. Place the ice cubes in the blender and whizz,
    then add the rest of the ingredients and
    blend until smooth.

2. Pour into a glass and garnish with
    sliced apricot and nectarine.

Red Silk

75 g/3 oz strawberries, hulled and chopped

75 g/3 oz raspberries

75 g/3 oz blackberries

150 ml/5 fl oz apple juice

Crushed ice to serve

Extra raspberries and blackberries
to garnish

1. Place all of the fruits and juice in the blender
   and blend until smooth.

2. Pour into a glass over ice and garnish with
   raspberries and blackberries.

Pineapple Pleasure

4 ice cubes

1 pear, peeled, quartered and cored

**½ medium-sized pineapple, peeled,
core and eyes removed and flesh
cut into chunks**

**8 large fresh mint leaves, plus
extra to garnish**

1. Place the ice cubes in the blender and whizz, then add the rest of the ingredients and blend until smooth.

2. Pour into a glass and garnish with mint.

Watermelon Wonder

450 g/1 lb watermelon, peeled, deseeded if preferred and cut into chunks

1 lime, peeled and halved

1 sprig fresh rosemary, needles only

Ice cubes to serve

1 chunk watermelon

Fresh rosemary to garnish

1. Place the watermelon, lime and rosemary in the blender and blend until smooth.

2. Pour into a glass over ice cubes and garnish.

Melon Magic

350 g/12 oz Honeydew melon, peeled,
deseeded and cut into chunks

2 kiwi fruits, peeled and quartered

4 lychees, peeled and stoned

Extra kiwi fruit to garnish

1. Place all of the ingredients in the blender
   and blend until smooth.

2. Pour into a glass and serve chilled,
   garnished with kiwi fruit.

Berry Banana Blast

150 g/5 oz blackberries

150 g/5 oz blueberries

1 banana, peeled and cut into chunks

225 ml/8 fl oz apple juice

Ice cubes to serve

Extra blackberries and blueberries
to garnish

1. Place the fruits and juice in the blender
and blend until smooth.

2. Pour into a glass over ice and garnish.

Cranberry Craving

150 ml/5 fl oz fresh orange juice

125 g/4½ oz natural yogurt

110 g/4 oz cranberries

150 g/5 oz raspberries

Ice cubes to serve

Fresh mint leaves to garnish

1. Place the orange juice and yogurt into the blender, then add the berries and blend until smooth.

2. Pour into a glass over ice and garnish.

Kiwi Kiss

2 kiwi fruit, peeled and quartered

Juice of ½ lime

175 g/6 oz strawberries, hulled

125 g/4½ oz strawberry-flavoured soya yogurt

100 ml/3½ fl oz non-dairy milk

Ice cubes to serve

Slice of kiwi fruit to garnish

1. Place the kiwi fruit, lime juice, strawberries, yogurt and milk in the blender and blend until smooth.

2. Pour into a glass over ice and garnish with a slice of kiwi fruit.

Papaya Passion

125 g/4½ oz live yogurt

1 papaya, peeled and deseeded

½ medium pineapple, core and eyes
removed and flesh cut into chunks

1.5 cm/½ in piece fresh ginger, peeled
and chopped

Ice cubes to serve

1. Put the yogurt into the blender first, then add the papaya, pineapple and ginger. Blend until smooth.

2. Pour into a glass over ice.

Berry Dazzler

4 ice cubes

150 g/5 oz cranberries

150 g/5 oz blueberries

100 ml/3½ fl oz pear juice

Extra cranberries and blueberries to garnish

1. Place the ice cubes in the blender and whizz.

2. Add the rest of the ingredients
and blend until smooth.

3. Pour into a glass and serve chilled,
garnished with extra cranberries and blueberries.

Jewels

1 pomegranate, halved and deseeded

1 passion-fruit, halved and pulp scooped out

3 Tbsp live yogurt

1. Carefully blend the pomegranate seeds, then strain through a fine mesh strainer.

2. Stir in passion-fruit pulp and yogurt.

Coconut Dream

2 handfuls strawberries, hulled

1 banana, peeled

2 Tbsp coconut milk

4 ice cubes

1. Juice the strawberries. Transfer to a blender with the banana, coconut milk and ice. Blend thoroughly.

2. Serve topped with freshly shaved coconut if desired.

Fruit & Veg

Green as Grass

150 g/5½ oz carrots

2 apples

Handful of wheatgrass, weighing about 50 g/2 oz

1. Top and tail the carrots and cut into chunks.
Remove the stalks from the apples and cut the fruit
into quarters. If the blades of wheatgrass are long,
snip them into shorter lengths with scissors.

2. Juice the carrots, apples and wheatgrass
together and pour into glasses.

On Your Marks

3 apples

115 g/4 oz spinach leaves

1 green pepper

1 celery stick with leaves

1 cm/⅜ in piece of fresh ginger

1. Remove the stalks from the apples and cut into quarters. Chop any large spinach leaves. Thickly slice the pepper leaving in the seeds. Cut the celery into short lengths and slice the ginger thinly without peeling.

2. Juice all the ingredients together. Pour into glasses and serve.

Red Giant

2 apples

150 g/5½ oz red cabbage

2 celery sticks with leaves

1 beetroot, weighing about 150 g/5½ oz

Ice and thin apple slices, to garnish

1. Remove the stalks from the apples and cut into quarters. Shred the red cabbage or cut into wedges small enough to fit down the feeder tube of the juicer. Cut the celery into short lengths and the beetroot into small wedges.

2. Juice the apples, red cabbage, celery and beetroot.

3. Pour into glasses half-filled with ice cubes or crushed ice and serve garnished with thin apple slices.

Veg Out

· ·

1 large sweet potato

1 apple

200 g/7 oz carrots

6 spears of tenderstem broccoli or 75 g/2½ oz small broccoli florets

A few fresh mint leaves to garnish

1. Cut the unpeeled sweet potato into chunks. Remove the stalk from the apple and cut into quarters. Top and tail the carrots and cut into chunks.

2. Juice the sweet potato, apple, carrots and broccoli.

3. Pour into glasses and garnish with a few mint leaves.

Carrot and Mango Crush

100 ml/3½ fl oz fresh orange juice

1 mango, halved either side of the stone, the flesh
scooped out and cut away from the stone

75 g/3 oz carrots, trimmed and chopped

Crushed ice to serve

Extra mango slice, to garnish

1. Place the orange juice and mango
   in the blender and blend, then add
   the carrots and blend until smooth.

2. Pour into a glass over crushed ice and garnish.

Wizard Juice

400 g/14 oz wedge of pumpkin

2 large oranges

Lightly toasted pumpkin seeds to serve

1. Peel the pumpkin and scrape out the seeds and fibres clinging to them. Cut the pumpkin flesh into small pieces or it will be hard to push through the juicer. Cut the rind away from the oranges, leaving the pith attached to the flesh. Cut into chunks.

2. Juice the pumpkin and oranges together and pour into glasses.

3. Sprinkle a few toasted pumpkin seeds on top and serve at once.

Red

1 head chicory

1 carrot top and bottom removed, choppped

1 red pepper stem removed, deseeded
and chopped

1. Juice chicory, carrot and
red pepper together. Stir.

Hot Beets

2 beetroot with leaves

1 celery stick with leaves, trimmed

2 cloves garlic, peeled

2 carrots, tops and bottoms removed

1. Juice all the ingredients. Combine.

Maple Butter

300 g/10½ oz butternut squash, peeled
and chopped

1 tsp maple syrup

1 Tbsp fresh thyme leaves

100 ml/3½ fl oz whole milk

1. Juice the squash. Blend with remaining
ingredients and drink immediately,
while bits of thyme are suspended throughout.

Terracotta

1 sweet potato, chopped

1 orange, peeled and halved

1 banana, peeled

1. Juice the sweet potato and orange.

2. Blend with the banana.

Stigma

½ head celeriac, scrubbed well and chopped

3 celery sticks, trimmed

Pinch of saffron, soaked in 1 tsp hot water

1. Juice the celeriac, then celery and blend together. Stir in saffron and its liquid.

Creamy Crimson

2 beetroots, tops and bottoms removed

100 ml/3½ fl oz live yogurt

1 tsp mustard seeds, plus an extra pinch
for sprinkling

1. Juice the beetroot. Blend with the remaining
   ingredients and serve with a sprinkling
   of mustard seeds on top.

Scarlet Woman

250 g/8 oz ripe tomatoes, quartered

8 large fresh basil leaves

3 spring onions, trimmed

1 red pepper, halved and deseeded

Crushed ice to serve

Fresh basil leaves to garnish

Salt and black pepper to taste

1. Place the tomatoes, basil leaves, onions and pepper in the blender and blend until smooth.

2. Pour into a glass over ice and garnish with basil leaves. You may like to add seasoning to taste.

Carrot Avocado Cleanser

250 g/8 oz carrots, trimmed

½ avocado, peeled, stoned and
cut into chunks

110 g/4 oz beansprouts

125 g/4½ oz natural yogurt

Ice cubes to serve

Carrot sticks to garnish

1. Juice the carrots. Put the juice into the blender
with the avocado, beansprouts and yogurt
and blend until smooth.

2. Pour into a glass over ice and garnish.

Flamenco Fool

225 ml/8 fl oz still mineral water, chilled

2 red peppers, roasted, quartered,
deseeded and skinned

125 g/4½ oz natural yogurt

50 g/2 oz sun-dried tomatoes, chopped

Salt and pepper, to taste

Ice cubes to serve

Fresh basil leaves to garnish

1. Place the water in the blender first,
then add the peppers, yogurt, sun-dried tomatoes
and seasoning. Blend.

2. Pour into a glass over ice and
garnish with basil leaves.

Beetroot Bliss

125 g/4½ oz cooked beetroot, cut into chunks

125 g/4½ oz natural yogurt

1 clove garlic, peeled and chopped

10 g/½ oz fresh chives, chopped

100 ml/3½ fl oz apple juice

Extra fresh chives to garnish

1. Place all of the ingredients in a blender
   and blend until smooth.

2. Pour into a glass and garnish
   with chives.

Green Ginger

½ green melon, peeled and deseeded

2 celery sticks, trimmed

1 cm/⅓ in piece fresh ginger, peeled

1. Juice the melon. Juice the celery and ginger together. Combine.

Liquid Thai

2 carrots, tops and bottoms removed

1 handful of fresh coriander

125 ml/4 fl oz coconut milk

1. Juice the carrots. Blend with coriander and coconut milk.

Avocado Ice

¼ iceberg lettuce, outer leaves removed

1 lime, peeled

¼ cucumber

½ avocado, peeled and stoned

1 tsp wasabi (optional)

3 ice cubes

1. Juice the lettuce, lime and cucumber. Transfer to a blender and blend with the avocado and wasabi.

2. Serve over ice.

Rejuvenator

6 radishes with leaves

1 lemon, peeled

3 carrots, tops and bottoms removed

1. Juice all the ingredients together. Stir.

Red Mist

150 g/5½ oz red cabbage, plus a little
extra to garnish

1 large pear

225 g/8 oz carrots, plus a little extra to garnish

1. Discard any discoloured outer leaves from
the cabbage and cut away any tough stalk or core.
Shred or cut the cabbage into wedges small enough
to fit down the feeder tube of the juicer. Twist the
stalk off the pear and cut into quarters or wedges.
Top and tail the carrots and cut into chunks.

2. Juice the cabbage, pear and carrots and pour
into glasses. Garnish with whisker-thin shreds of
cabbage and a little grated carrot.

Up-Beet

225 g/8 oz carrots

1 medium beetroot

115 g/4oz watercress

1 cm/⅓ in piece of fresh ginger

1. Top, tail and chop the carrots, cut the beetroot into small wedges (reserving any small leaves for garnish) and discard any yellow watercress leaves. Thinly slice the ginger, leaving the skin on unless it is shrivelled.

2. Juice the vegetables and ginger and pour into small glasses. Serve garnished with any reserved beetroot leaves.

Agent Orange

½ papaya, weighing about 300 g/10½ oz

3 large oranges, plus extra wedges to serve

2 celery sticks with leaves, plus extra leaves to garnish

1. Scoop the seeds out of the papaya and chop the unpeeled flesh. Cut the rind away from the oranges, leaving the pith attached to the flesh, and chop. Cut the celery into short lengths.

2. Juice the papaya, oranges and celery and pour into glasses. Garnish with orange wedges and celery leaves and serve.

Red Alert

750 g/1 lb 10 oz ripe tomatoes

85 g/3 oz carrots

1 celery stick with leaves

Extra carrot or celery sticks to serve

1. Halve the tomatoes. Top, tail and chop the carrots into chunks. Cut the celery into 5 cm/2 in lengths.

2. Juice the vegetables and pour into glasses. Garnish with a celery or carrot stick as the juice separates quite quickly and this can be used to give it a good stir before drinking.

Cucumber Cooler

200 g/7 oz cucumber

110 g/4 oz fennel bulb, outer part removed,

cut into chunks

150 g/5 oz tender asparagus, trimmed

Ice cubes to serve

1 sprig fennel frond to garnish

1. Juice the cucumber, fennel and asparagus together.
Pour into a glass over ice. Garnish.

Carrot Crazy

175 g/6 oz carrots, trimmed

2 celery sticks, trimmed

1 apple, quartered and cored

Crushed ice to serve

1. Juice the carrots, celery and apple together.
   Pour into a glass over crushed ice.

Cleansers & Energisers

Floo Fighter

2 lemons, peeled
1 cm/⅓ in piece fresh ginger, peeled
200 ml/7 fl oz chamomile tea, chilled

1. Juice the lemons and ginger together.

2. Add the chamomile tea and stir.

Tender Tummy

½ fennel, outer part removed

2 apples, halved and cored

Pinch of ground ginger

1. Juice the fennel and apples separately.

2. Add fennel juice to apple juice, to taste. Sprinkle ginger on top. Stir.

Goggles

1 carrot, top and bottom removed, chopped

2 sticks celery, chopped

1 small fennel bulb, halved
and leafy tops removed

1. Juice the carrot, celery and fennel together. Stir.

Bright and Breezy

40 g/1½ oz watercress

115 g/4 oz green cabbage

1 apple

1 orange pepper

1 Tbsp chopped fresh parsley

1. Remove any yellow leaves from the watercress. Roughly chop the cabbage leaves. Twist the stalk off the apple and cut into quarters. Cut the pepper into thick slices without removing the seeds.

2. Juice the watercress, cabbage, apple and pepper.

3. Stir in the parsley, pour into glasses and serve.

Hot Recharge

1 yellow pepper, stalk removed, deseeded

1 red pepper, stalk removed, deseeded

1 red chilli, seeds and membrane removed

1 bunch spinach, tough stalks removed, chopped

1. Juice the yellow pepper. Juice the red pepper and chilli together. Finally, juice the spinach and add to the pepper juices. Stir before drinking.

Spring Clean

2 medium carrots

¼ cucumber, weighing about 125 g/4½ oz

1 small beetroot, weighing about 75 g/2½ oz

2 celery sticks with leaves

Crushed ice

Small fresh dill sprigs, to garnish

1. Top and tail the carrots and chop into chunks. Cut the cucumber into short lengths. Cut the beetroot into small wedges. Chop the celery into short lengths.

2. Juice all the vegetables together.

3. Serve poured over crushed ice and garnish with a few small sprigs of dill.

Morning Loosener

2 pears, cored and quartered

1 apple, cored and quartered

8 prunes

1. Juice the pears and apple together.

2. Transfer to a blender and add the prunes. Blend thoroughly.

Carrot Charger

3 carrots, tops and bottoms removed

1 orange, peeled

2 tsp spirulina powder

1 tsp sesame seeds

1. Juice the carrots and orange.

2. Stir in the spirulina and sesame seeds.

Bright Eyes

225 g/8 oz carrots

1 apple

2 oranges

2 Tbsp chopped fresh parsley

1. Top, tail and chop the carrots. Twist the stalk off the apple and cut into quarters. Cut the rind off the oranges using a vegetable peeler.

2. Juice the carrots, apple and oranges, pour into glasses and sprinkle the parsley on top.

Pick-Me-Up

2 oranges, peeled

8 fresh mint leaves

1 lime, peeled

1 passion-fruit, halved and pulp scooped out

1. Juice the oranges, mint and lime together.

2. Stir in the passion-fruit pulp and serve with a sprig of mint.

On the Beet

1 small beetroot

200 g/7 oz carrots, plus extra julienne
strips to garnish

1 potato, weighing about 225 g/8 oz

4 radishes

1. Cut the beetroot into small wedges. Top and tail
the carrots and chop into chunks. Cut the unpeeled
potato into chunks that will fit down the feeder
tube of the juicer. Top and tail the radishes.

2. Juice all the vegetables together,
pour into glasses and serve garnished
with julienne strips of carrot.

Pepper Plus

1 red pepper

1 medium carrot

1 medium orange

1. Thickly slice the pepper without removing the seeds. Top and tail the carrot and slice into chunks. Cut the rind away from the orange using a vegetable peeler, leaving the pith attached to the flesh, and chop.

2. Juice the pepper, carrot and orange together, pour into glasses and serve.

Prune Blast

4 large pitted prunes

1 peach

2 celery sticks with leaves

2 medium carrots

1. Soak the prunes in 100 ml/3½ fl oz boiling water for 1 hour. Purée the prunes with their soaking water in a blender. Halve the peach and remove the stone. Chop the celery into short lengths. Top and tail the carrots and cut into chunks.

2. Juice the peach, celery and carrots together and whisk or stir in the prune purée.

3. Pour into glasses and serve.

Go Green

2 bunches (about 200 g/7 oz) watercress

100 g/3½ oz spinach leaves

2 apples

2 celery sticks, with leaves

1. Discard any yellow watercress leaves and shred any large spinach leaves. Twist the stalks off the apples and quarter. Chop the celery.

2. Juice all the ingredients together in small batches to extract the maximum liquid from the watercress and spinach, keeping a few watercress leaves aside.

3. Pour into glasses and garnish with the reserved sprigs of watercress.

Royal Flush

1 beetroot with leaves

1 carrot, top and bottom removed, chopped

1 apple, cored and chopped

2cm/¾ in piece fresh ginger, peeled

Juice of ½ lime, peeled

1. Juice beetroot, carrot, apple, ginger and lime. Stir.

True Blue

1 apple

75 g/2½ oz blackcurrants

75 g/2½ oz blueberries

75 g/2½ oz blackberries

Ice cubes

1. Remove the stalk from the apple and cut into quarters. Pull the blackcurrants off their stalks.

2. Juice all the fruits together, pour into glasses and serve over ice.

Watercress Cooler

2 nashi pears

200 g/7 oz wedge of Galia or Ogen melon

75 g/2½ oz watercress

1. Remove the stalks from the nashi pears and cut into quarters or wedges. Peel the melon if the skin is hard and cut the flesh into chunks without removing the seeds. Pick any yellow leaves off the watercress.

2. Juice the pears, melon and watercress together, pour into glasses and serve.

Golden Glow

4 apricots

1 medium mango

2 peaches

2 large oranges

Shredded orange zest to garnish

1. Halve and stone the apricots.
Cut the unpeeled flesh of the mango away
from the stone. Halve, stone and slice the peaches
thickly. Cut the rind away from the oranges,
and cut into chunks.

2. Juice all the fruit and pour into glasses.

Cleansers & Energisers

Green Leaf

2 celery sticks with leaves

1 apple

125 g/4½ oz lettuce, eg Cos

75 g/2½ oz spinach leaves

75 g/2½ oz sugar snap peas

1. Cut the celery into short lengths. Remove the stalk from the apple and cut into quarters. Roughly tear up the lettuce leaves and chop any large spinach leaves.

2. Juice the celery, apple, lettuce, spinach and sugar snap peas together, pour into glasses and serve.

Groovy Ruby

1 small beetroot

3 large oranges

1. Cut the beetroot into small wedges. Cut the rind away from the oranges, leaving the pith attached to the flesh. Chop into chunks and juice the oranges with the beetroot.

2. Pour into glasses and serve.

Sweet Red

2 handfuls raspberries (fresh or frozen)

2 handfuls cranberries (fresh or frozen)

½ stalk lemongrass, trimmed and chopped

1 Tbsp elderflower cordial

175 ml/6 fl oz mineral water (still or sparkling)

1. Juice the raspberries, cranberries and lemongrass together.

2. Make up the elderflower cordial with the water in a tumbler. Pour the cordial over the berry juice and stir.

Power Punch

2 bunches spinach, tough stalks removed, and chopped

2 celery sticks, trimmed

1 clove garlic, peeled

Pinch of cayenne

150 ml/5 fl oz still mineral water

1. Juice the spinach, celery and garlic.

2. Stir in the cayenne and mineral water.

Golden Girl

450 g/1 lb rhubarb

1 large orange

2 medium carrots

1 cm/½ in piece of fresh ginger

Mineral water (optional)

1. Cut the rhubarb into short lengths,
discarding any leaves as these are poisonous.
Cut the rind away from the orange, leaving the pith
attached to the flesh, and chop into chunks.
Top and tail the carrots and cut into chunks.
Thinly slice the unpeeled ginger.

2. Juice the rhubarb, orange, carrots and ginger.

3. Pour into glasses and dilute with mineral water
if you find the consistency too thick.

Coral

2 apples, cored and quartered

1 handful of raspberries

1 handful of strawberries, hulled

10 drops panax ginseng extract

1. Juice the apples.
Blend with the raspberries and strawberries.

2. Stir in the ginseng extract.

Tuscan Nectar

2 handfuls (approx. 30) seedless grapes

2 fresh figs, stalks removed and halved

Juice of ½ a lemon

1. Juice the grapes, then the figs.
Stir in the lemon juice.

Sweet Fortification

2 nectarines, halved and stoned

1 peach, halved and stoned

5 strawberries, hulled

5 drops echinacea extract

1. Juice the nectarines and peach together.

2. Blend with the strawberries and echinacea.

Relax

Just Relax

½ cucumber

100 g/ 3½ oz carrots

1 celery stick with leaves

½ small pineapple, about 400 g/14 oz
unpeeled weight

Celery sticks and pineapple leaves, to garnish

1. Cut the cucumber into chunks. Top, tail and chop the carrots. Coarsely chop the celery and leaves. Peel the pineapple and cut into chunks.

2. Juice the vegetables and pineapple, pour into glasses and serve garnished with celery sticks and pineapple leaves.

Fig Fix

1 orange, peeled

2 fresh figs, stalk removed and halved

1 vanilla pod, seeds scooped out

6 Tbsp live yogurt

2 tsp honey

1. Juice the orange. Transfer to a blender and blend with the remaining ingredients (use only the vanilla seeds, discard the pod or put it into a container filled with caster sugar to add a vanilla flavour to your baking).

Chill Out

115 g/4 oz spinach leaves

2 pears

50 g/2 oz watercress, plus extra sprigs to garnish

1. Coarsely chop any large spinach leaves. Twist the stalks off the pears and cut the fruit into quarters. Discard any yellow watercress leaves.

2. Juice the spinach, pears and watercress and pour into glasses. Serve garnished with small watercress sprigs.

Berry Nice

115 g/4 oz strawberries

115 g/4 oz raspberries

115 g/4 oz blackberries

115 g/4 oz blueberries

A few extra berries, to garnish

1. Juice all the berries together. Pour into glasses and serve garnished with extra fruits.

Honeymoon Cocktail

Crushed ice

1 part apple juice

1 part fresh orange juice

Squeeze of fresh lime juice

2 tsp runny honey

Orange peel and a maraschino cherry,
to garnish

1. Place a scoop of crushed ice in a cocktail shaker,
add the apple and orange juices, squeeze over
the lime and pour in the honey. Shake well
and strain into two Champagne flutes.
Garnish with a spiral of orange peel and a cherry.

In the Mood

½ Cantaloupe melon

1 large orange

1 banana

2 figs

1. Cut the unpeeled melon into chunks small enough to fit down the feeder tube of the juicer. Cut the rind away from the orange using a vegetable peeler, leaving the pith attached to the flesh. Slice or cut into chunks. Peel and cut the banana into three or four pieces.

2. Juice the melon and orange with one fig. Pour into a blender, add the banana and liquidise until smooth.

3. Pour into glasses, cut the remaining fig into slices and use to garnish the drinks.

Night Cap

2 apples

1 lemon

1 orange

Small piece of cinnamon stick

Hot water

1–2 tsp clear honey, or to taste

Extra orange wedges and apple slices to garnish

1. Twist the stalks off the apples and cut the fruit into quarters. Shave the rind off the lemon and orange and roughly chop the flesh. Juice all the fruit and chill until needed.

2. When ready to serve, half fill a glass or mug with juice, add a small piece of cinnamon stick and top up with hot water. Stir in clear honey to taste. Serve garnished with orange wedges and apple slices and remove the cinnamon stick before drinking.

No Stress

175 g/6 oz green cabbage leaves

225 g/8 oz parsnips

1 small sweet potato

Ice cubes (optional)

1. Shred the cabbage leaves or cut into pieces that will fit easily down the feeder tube of the juicer. Cut the parsnips and sweet potato to fit as well – neither needs peeling.

2. Juice all the vegetables and pour into chilled glasses or serve over ice.

Melon Breeze

½ Ogen or Cantaloupe melon

½ mini watermelon, weighing about 675 g/1 lb 8 oz

1 small lemon or ½ large lemon

Ice cubes (optional)

Shredded mint leaves, to garnish

1. Cut the melons into chunks without removing the peel or the seeds. Peel the lemon, leaving on the pith, and remove the seeds.

2. Juice all the fruit together, reserving a few small pieces of watermelon for garnish, and adjusting the flavour by adding extra lemon juice if preferred. Pour into chilled glasses or serve over ice. Garnish with the reserved watermelon and sprinkle with a little finely shredded mint.

Pink Panther

700 g/1 lb 9 oz wedge of Honeydew melon

8 lychees

175 g/6 oz strawberries

125 g/4½ oz raspberries

1. Cut the unpeeled melon into chunks without removing the seeds. Peel the lychees and remove the seeds. Cut any large strawberries in half – there's no need to hull them.

2. Juice the melon, lychees, strawberries and raspberries. Pour into glasses and serve.

Blackberry Pie

2 handfuls blackberries

2 apples, cored and quartered

Pinch of ground cinnamon

1. Juice the blackberries and apples together. Stir in the cinnamon. Serve cool or warm it over a moderate heat.

Maple Marvel

3 plums, halved and stoned

2 pinches of ground cinnamon

6 Tbsp live yogurt

2 Tbsp maple syrup

1. Juice the plums. Stir in the remaining ingredients and mix thoroughly.

Pacific Perfection

¼ pineapple, peeled

½ mango, peeled and stoned

2 passion-fruits, flesh scooped out

1. Juice the pineapple and mango. Stir in the passion-fruit.

Sage Citrus

2 oranges, peeled

1 lemon, peeled

6 fresh sage leaves

4 ice cubes

1. Juice the oranges, lemon and sage together.
Pour over ice.

Crocus Milk

Pinch of saffron, soaked in 1 tsp hot water

1 banana, peeled

125 ml/4 fl oz full-fat milk

1. Blend ingredients together.

Perfect Pair

2 pears, halved and cored

1 Tbsp pine nuts, toasted

1. Juice the pears. Blend with toasted pine nuts.

Relax

Orange Blossom

2 apricots, halved and stoned

2 peaches, halved and stoned

1 splash orange flower water

1. Juice the apricots and peaches together.

2. Add a splash of orange flower water and stir.

Convalescent

2 handfuls grapes

1 papaya, peeled and seeds scooped out

Juice of ½ lemon

1. Juice the grapes, papaya and lemon. Stir.

Citrus City

1 grapefruit, peeled

1 orange, peeled

Juice of ½ lemon

Juice of ½ lime

1. Juice the grapefruit, orange, lemon and lime. Stir.

Tomato Tonic

4 tomatoes, stalks removed

1 clove garlic, peeled

6 fresh sage leaves

1 Tbsp runny honey

3 ice cubes

1. Juice the tomatoes, garlic and sage together.

2. Stir in the honey thoroughly and pour over ice.

Chill Out Lemon

2 large lemons

2–3 Tbsp caster sugar, or to taste

Still mineral or tap water

4 large or 8 small scoops of lemon sorbet

1. Cut the lemons into chunks and place in a blender with 2 tablespoons caster sugar. Blend until smooth.

2. Strain into a measuring jug, pushing as much of the pulp as you can through the strainer with a wooden spoon. Taste the juice and add more sugar to taste, although remember the lemon sorbet will also sweeten it. Top up to 500 ml/18 fl oz with still water.

3. Pour into tumblers and add one or two scoops of lemon sorbet to each. Allow the sorbet to melt a little before drinking.

Hot Orange Spiced Tea

1 large lemon

1 large orange

850 ml/1½ pt water

4–5 cloves

1 stick of cinnamon

3 green tea bags

Honey or sugar to taste

Cinnamon sticks and orange slices to serve

1. Squeeze the juice from the lemon and the orange –
about 3 tablespoons lemon juice and 75 ml/3 fl oz orange juice.

2. Put the water, cloves and cinnamon in a saucepan and bring
to the boil. Remove from the heat, leave to stand for 1 minute,
then add the tea bags. Set aside to infuse for 5 minutes.

3. Remove the tea bags and, if sweetening, stir in honey
or sugar to taste. Strain in the lemon and orange juices and
reheat gently. Serve with cinamon sticks and orange slices.

Winter Warmer

2 pears, quartered and cored

1 apple, quartered and cored

2 star anise

1. Juice the fruit together and pour into a saucepan.

2. Add the star anise. Bring slowly to the boil and allow to infuse. Pour into a glass and serve warm.

Chamomile Calm

200 ml/7 fl oz cold chamomile tea
(use 2 tea bags)

1 papaya, peeled, halved and deseeded

Ice cubes to serve

1. Put the chamomile tea and papaya
in the blender and blend until smooth.
Pour into a glass over ice.

Cool Down Cordial

2 apples, plus extra to garnish

350 g/12½ oz plums

100 g/3½ oz blackberries

1. Twist the stalks off the apples and cut the fruit into quarters. Remove the stalks from the plums, halve and take out the stones.

2. Juice the apples, plums and blackberries. Pour into glasses and garnish each serving with extra apple cut into julienne (thin) strips.

Blue Spice

1 orange, peeled

3 handfuls blueberries

1 apple, cored and quartered

2 pinches of ground nutmeg

Pinch of ground cinnamon

1. Juice the orange, blueberries and apple.
   Stir in the nutmeg and cinnamon.

Celebrate & Indulge

Malibu Cooler

½ pineapple, peeled

1 Tbsp ground almonds

2 Tbsp coconut milk

3 ice cubes

1. Juice the pineapple.

2. Stir in the almonds and coconut milk. Pour over ice.

Grape Spritzer

1 bunch white grapes, stalks removed

1 tsp elderflower cordial

175 ml/6 fl oz sparkling mineral water

3 ice cubes

1. Juice the grapes.

2. Add the elderflower cordial and water. Pour over ice.

Passionate Peach

2 peaches, halved and stoned

8 fresh mint leaves, chopped

2 passion-fruit, halved and pulp scooped out

4 ice cubes

1. Juice the peach and mint together.

2. Add the passion-fruit pulp and pour over ice. Serve with a sprig of mint.

Cairns Cooler

Ice cubes

1 part canned pineapple juice

1 part fresh orange juice

½ part coconut cream

1 bar measure of sugar syrup (about an egg cup)

Thin slice of pineapple and maraschino cherry,

to garnish

Place about six ice cubes in a cocktail shaker,
add the pineapple and orange juices, coconut
cream and sugar syrup, and shake well.
Strain into a highball glass and garnish with a slice
of pineapple, if available, and a cherry on a stick.

Mango Lush

1 mango, peeled and stoned

½ stalk lemongrass, trimmed and chopped
0.5 cm/¼ in piece fresh ginger, peeled

1 apple, cored and quartered

1. Juice all the ingredients together.

Raspberry Zinger

3 handfuls raspberries

1 lime, peeled

2 oranges, peeled

6 fresh mint leaves

3 ice cubes

1. Juice the raspberries, lime and oranges together.

2. Chop the mint finely and combine. Pour over ice cubes.

Heaven Scent

8 lychees, peeled

1 tsp rosewater

2–3 ice cubes

1 tsp grenadine

1. Blend the lychees with the rosewater and ice.

2. Pour in grenadine.

Strawberry Must

2 handfuls strawberries, hulled

2 tsp balsamic vinegar

75 ml/3 fl oz cream

Honey to taste

1–2 ice cubes

1. Blend the strawberries.

2. Pour in the balsamic vinegar, cream and honey to taste. Serve over ice.

Fantasia

6 strawberries, rinsed and hulled

Slice of Honeydew melon, rind removed

1 part fresh orange juice

1 part pineapple juice

1 part crushed ice

Thin slice of pineapple, to garnish

1. Place five of the strawberries, the melon, and the orange and pineapple juices in a blender and blend to a smooth consistency.

2. Place the crushed ice in a highball glass and pour the blended mixture over it. Garnish with the remaining strawberry, sliced in half and a slice of pineapple, if available.

Surfers' Paradise

Crushed ice

Juice of 1 fresh lime

2 dashes of Angostura bitters

Lemonade

Slice of lime, to garnish

1. Place a scoop of crushed ice in a highball glass and pour the lime juice, bitters and lemonade over it.

2. Stir gently and decorate with a slice of lime.

Cranberry Sparkler

Crushed ice

1 part cranberry juice

1 part fresh lemon juice

1 part soda water

Slice of lemon, to garnish

1. Fill a highball glass with crushed ice and pour the cranberry and lemon juices, and soda water over it. Stir gently.

2. Garnish with a slice of lemon.

Virgin Mary

Ice cubes

1 can tomato juice

2 Tbsp fresh lemon juice

2 dashes of Worcestershire sauce

2 drops of Tabasco sauce

Pinch of celery salt

Salt and pepper, to taste

Celery stick

1. Place a scoop of ice cubes in a cocktail shaker, then add all the ingredients, except for the celery stick, and shake well.

2. Strain into a lowball glass and use the celery stick as a stirrer.

Banana Bomb

1 ripe banana

1 whole egg

1 Tbsp runny honey

Enough chilled full-fat milk to fill the glass

1. Cut the banana into chunks and place in a blender. Add the egg, honey and milk, and blend to a smooth milkshake consistency.

2. Serve in a tall glass. (For those who hesitate at the thought of including a raw egg, this can be omitted, although it does reduce the richness.)

Passion

1 banana

Juice of 1 orange, mixed with an equal quantity
of mango juice

2 dessertspoons passion fruit pulp

Ice cubes

Maraschino cherry, to garnish

1. Cut the banana into chunks and
place in a blender.

2. Add the orange and mango juices, and passion
fruit pulp and blend for about 10 seconds.

3. Fill a highball glass with ice cubes and pour the
fruit juice mix over it. Garnish with a cherry on a stick.

Grecian Lady

Crushed ice

4 parts peach juice

2 parts orange juice

1 part fresh lemon juice

Soda water

Fruit slices or stoned cherries, to garnish

1. Place a scoop of crushed ice in a cocktail shaker and add the peach, orange and lemon juices.

2. Shake well and strain into a large wine glass.

3. Add a squirt of soda water to fill the glass and decorate with slices of fruit or stoned cherries threaded on a cocktail stick.

Jungle Cooler

Crushed ice

4 parts pineapple juice

2 parts fresh orange juice

1 part passion-fruit squash or cordial

1 part coconut milk

Slice of pineapple, to garnish

1. Place a scoop of crushed ice in a cocktail shaker and add the pineapple, orange and passion fruit juices along with the coconut milk. Shake well and strain into a tall glass.

2. Garnish with a slice of pineapple and serve.

Celebrate & Indulge

Ginger Snap

Crushed ice

1 part fresh orange juice

1 part grapefruit juice

1 part cranberry juice

2 tsp ginger marmalade

½ tsp ground ginger or fresh grated ginger

Slice of orange, to garnish

1. Place a scoop of crushed ice in a cocktail shaker and add the orange, grapefruit and cranberry juices, ginger marmalade and the ground or grated ginger.

2. Shake well, strain into a tall glass and garnish with a slice of orange.

Silver Sour

1 egg white

Ice cubes

Juice of 1 large lemon

Equal quantity of thick apricot juice or purée

1 tsp caster sugar

Soda water

2 slices of green apple, to garnish

1. Place the egg white in a cocktail shaker with four ice cubes, the lemon juice and apricot juice or purée.

2. Add the sugar (or adjust to taste) and shake well for about 10 seconds. Strain into a wine goblet and top up with soda water.

3. Stir gently and decorate with a couple of apple slices on the rim of the glass.

Grape Sparkler

2 whole white grapes

2 whole black grapes

Squeeze of lemon juice

Sparkling white grape juice, well chilled

1. Thread the white and black grapes alternately on a long cocktail stick and stand it upright in a Champagne flute.

2. Squeeze a little lemon juice over them and fill the glass with sparkling grape juice.

Yankee Flip

Ice cubes

1 egg yolk

1 tsp caster sugar

1 part pineapple juice

2 parts red grape juice

Grated nutmeg to serve

1. Place five or six ice cubes in a cocktail shaker and add the egg yolk, sugar, pineapple and grape juices.

2. Shake thoroughly until smoothly blended and strain into a wine glass.

3. Grate a sprinkling of nutmeg over it and serve.

Virgin Sea Breeze

Ice cubes

1 part cranberry juice

1 part grapefruit juice

1. Fill a highball glass with ice cubes, pour the cranberry and grapefruit juices over the ice, stir gently and serve ungarnished.

Summer Soda

Juice of 1 orange

Juice of 1 lemon

Juice of 1 grapefruit

Ice cubes

Soda water

Scoop of soft vanilla ice cream

Glacé cherry, to garnish

1. Pour the orange, lemon and grapefruit juices in a cocktail shaker with five or six ice cubes and shake.

2. Strain into a tall glass, filling it to the halfway mark. Top up to almost full with soda water and add a scoop of vanilla ice cream. Top with a cherry and serve with a straw and long-handled spoon.

Fun-Gria

Lemon juice and caster sugar, for frosting

Ice cubes

1 part fresh orange juice

1 part red grape juice

Generous squeeze of lemon juice

Orange zest

Slice of lemon, to garnish

1. Rub the rim of a large wine glass with lemon juice then dip it into a saucer of caster sugar to frost the rim.

2. Place four ice cubes in a shaker, add the orange and grape juices and the lemon juice.

3. Shake well and strain into the frosted glass. Add a sprinkling of orange zest and garnish with a slice of lemon.

Cinderella

Ice cubes

1 part canned pineapple juice

1 part fresh lemon juice

1 part fresh orange juice

Dash of grenadine

Soda water

Slice of pineapple to garnish

1. Place five or six ice cubes in a cocktail shaker and pour in the pineapple, lemon and orange juices, and grenadine.

2. Shake well and strain into a tall glass.

3. Top up with soda water and garnish with a slice of pineapple.

Island Romance

1 slice fresh, ripe Honeydew melon

Crushed ice

Juice of 1 large orange

Equal quantity of coconut milk

Equal quantity of mango juice

1 Tbsp whipped cream

1. Peel and cut the melon into chunks. Place the pieces in a blender with a scoop of crushed ice and blend to a purée. Place this carefully into a Champagne flute, filling it to about one third.

2. Now float the coconut milk on top of it, followed by the orange and mango juices, trying to keep them separate (not essential, but it's fun to try!).

3. Top with whipped cream and serve.

Plum Joy

2 large, very ripe plums

Crushed ice

Juice of ½ lemon

2 Tbsp sugar syrup

2 Tbsp plum jam

Sparkling bitter lemon

1. Peel the plums and cut into smallish pieces.
Place them in a blender with a scoop of crushed
ice and a couple of spoons of cold water.
Add the lemon juice, sugar syrup and plum jam,
and blend to a smooth purée.

2. Strain this into a tall glass and top up with the
bitter lemon. Stir gently to blend and serve.

Index

Acknowledgments

Our thanks to:

David Biggs; pp. 265, 267, 269, 271, 273, 275, 277, 279, 281, 283, 285, 287, 289, 291, 293, 295, 297, 299

Pippa Cuthbert and Lindsay Cameron-Wilson; pp. 57, 59, 153, 233, 245, 249, 285, 253, 257, 259, 261, 263, 81, 101, 103, 105, 107, 109, 119, 121, 123, 125, 141, 143, 145, 149, 155, 159, 169, 181, 183, 187, 189, 191, 197, 215, 217, 219, 221, 223, 225, 229, 231

Stella Murphy; pp. 33, 35, 37, 39, 41, 43, 45, 47, 61, 63, 67, 69, 71, 73, 75, 77, 79, 111, 113, 115, 117, 135, 137, 239, 241

Wendy Sweetser; 49, 51, 53, 55, 87, 89, 91, 93, 95, 97, 133, 127, 129, 131, 147, 151, 157, 161, 163, 165, 167, 171, 173, 177, 179, 185, 175, 195, 199, 201, 205, 207, 209, 211, 213, 235, 237, 243